EXIT (TO LEAVE OR DEPART FROM A PLACE OR SITUATION) PLAN (TO DESIGN, OUTLINE OR ARRANGE IN ADVANCE)

by
Katrina "Trina" Frierson

Copyright © 2016 by Katrina Frierson

All rights reserved. This book or any portion thereof may not be reproduced or used in any manner whatsoever without the express written permission of the publisher except for the use of brief quotations in a book review.

Printed in the United States of America
Edited by Louise Grant.

Special thanks to my praying Mamma, Verta Mae Frierson, my kids Kenishea, Kewanna, Kevin and Kala, and my best friend for life Charlotte Grant.

Special thanks to the staff at CCA: Allie Marlow, Jennell Brown, Nita Keith and Chasa Leek.

We are so grateful to the Davidson County Sheriff's Office for allowing us to bring this *Exit Plan* 7-week program as a pilot classroom experience to a group of females who are incarcerated.

This book is dedicated to my "cellys" in hopes that you will find your way out of messed up situation to begin your journey of life that was designed for you by You/God.

TABLE OF CONTENTS

Foreword 5

Chapter 1 *Behind the Bars - Again* 7

Chapter 2 *Finding a Way into Treatment* 13

Chapter 3 *Finding The Parent Within Me* 19

Chapter 4 *Recognizing the Change That is Needed* 25

Chapter 5 *Setting Personal Goals* 31

Chapter 6 *Finding Hope* 37

Chapter 7 *Finding an Exit Strategy on the Road to Release* 43

Chapter 8 *Employment and Lifestyle Opportunities* 51

Chapter 9 *Being Honest With Ourselves* 57

Chapter 10 *Staying Strong and On the Path* 63

Chapter 11 *Your Personal Final Release Plan* 69

Final Thoughts *How I Made It* 79

> *"10 percent of the 600,000 people a year coming out of jails and prison have serious issues with the lack of housing. That's 60,000 people a year."*

FOREWORD

Understanding The Need To Fix a Problem

As an incarcerated individual, being mentally, spiritually and emotionally ready to change is more important than making that physical change to freedom outside those security fences that keep us locked in. If our minds are not internally prepared to move then our bodies tend to only have a presence in free society and will gravitate right back to that comfort zone of the past places and people.

Most of us who prepare to leave prisons and jails do not have a home, or at least not one that is the healthiest and most stable environment than can help us continue to heal and recover, which is always needed regardless of how many classes or rehabilitation programs we participated in while incarcerated. Too many times, we find ourselves going back to neighborhoods where housing, employment, transportation and healthy-living lifestyles are not at our finger tips. The lack of these necessities can serve to quickly put us in emotional jeopardy and at risk of repeating the cycle of crime.

CHAPTER 1

In this chapter, we look at the life of the author's personal past and see what in Trina's experiences led her to her repeated incarceration.

We review your personal history of crime and incarceration as a repeated offender.

You will start looking at early dreams for your life.

Behind the Bars - Again

In 1996 I received the last of my 17 criminal charges. Those severe charges dated back to the early 1990s and represented a time in my life that was filled with anger, drugs, apathy and despair.

I went to prison that same year, never imagining it would have been my last time. After all, I had been in and out of prison and jail time and time again. I couldn't imagine another way of living. And although I was released in 1997, it often feels as if it was yesterday instead of nearly 20 years ago. In my mind, I can hear the sound of those prison gates shutting and the buzz of the security officers' radios blaring into the late evening while I slept on my bunk. I can see the faces of my cellmates, some of them wracked with emotional pain, and others filled with anger. But, even in prison, most of the people there were relaxed, accepting, and even filled with hope and friendship.

While I do not miss being incarcerated, I do miss the people who challenged me to do something different with my life. There were people who challenged me to see myself as a person of worth and a person who had a purpose in life. For most of my prison time, I saw myself as simply a drug addict, a convict. Once you label yourself as just a criminal addict, it takes an enormous amount of effort to turn that belief system around.

> *Once you label yourself as just a criminal addict, it takes an enormous amount of effort to turn that belief system around.*

But our lives are important – every addict's life is of value; every hardened criminal's life has value. And our beliefs of lack and unworthiness are what really keeps us in shackles. Prison isn't what strips away our freedom. It's our lack of belief in ourselves that imprisons us.

Please understand that I'm not saying that jail is a good thing. Yes, it serves society in important ways, but for those of us who are placed there, it does not feel like a good thing. What I am saying, though, is that for some of us, spending time behind bars is exactly what we need in order to move forward in our lives and find that sense of internal freedom that can bring about a state of peace.

When I faced the criminal court system with a lengthy charge list, my charges ranged from possessions for resale, to carrying weapons, to assault. And there were so many drugs; those easily could have been part of the charge as well. The assault charges actually involved my own family members. Yes, things had gotten so bad within our family that we had actually started to fight one another, damage each other's vehicles, and even shoot each other. At the time, it didn't seem too dysfunctional or even that uncommon, based on the people I knew and connected with on the streets.

During that stage in my life, prison and jail sentences were just another extension of life. I can recall going to jail, getting out and trying to find a job and being rejected due to the felonies. I would give up in despair and repeat what I knew best, which was selling drugs and weapons.

My own heavy drug use put such a haze over my life that I could barely distinguish between legal and illegal activities. None of it mattered. During this painful cycle in my life, I would find myself right back in jail a few months after getting out. By this time, the intense fear that I'd faced during my first incarceration had evaporated, and I was fairly numb to the experience. I didn't view my life as one that was worth fighting for, so I just spent time instead fighting other people.

I look at my life growing up and know that my environment had so much to do with me being in prison. It's not an excuse, and I absolutely am accountable today for my criminal actions. But from such a young age,

I grew up in the poor, black neighborhoods near subsidized housing where drugs were commonplace, and violence was also. And even though I went to high school and found a connection to team sports, I allowed the drug use to play a starring role in my life instead of having me be the star athlete I could have been. And so it became a young life focused on drugs, sex and a need to belong.

1. How many times have you been incarcerated? _____

2. What are your charges? _____

3. Have other family members been incarcerated? What relation are they to you?_____

_____

4. What led you to your first crimes? _____

_____

5. Did your charges complicate employment for you? How? What did you do if you were rejected?

_____

_____

_____

6. Did you have any dreams for your life when you were younger? What were they?

_____

_____

_____

Chapter 1 Homework Assignment:

A. Are you still using your street mentality to survive in jail? If so, how is it expressing itself in your life? How does it affect others in the jail?

_____
_____
_____
_____
_____

B. What will your life look like if you continue your same old behavior when you are released?

_____
_____
_____
_____
_____

EXIT PLAN

CHAPTER 2

In this chapter, we experience Trina's courage to move into addictions treatment.

You will be challenged to look at any negative behaviors.

You will be able to share positive things about yourself.

Finding a Way into Treatment

I remember as if it was yesterday going to jail and doing an 18 month sentence. I was in housing unit "C." I lived across from the women who were in addictions treatment. They had decided they were tired of their lifestyle and wanted to find a new way of living that wouldn't continue to destroy their health, their hope and the hopes of their families. Emotionally, I was not at all where they were. I would mess with them, saying what I could to create conflict and doubt in their minds.

"Man, ya'll are like getting brain washed in there," I would say to those ladies in treatment.

"Ya'll know you're going to be doing the same thing when you get out," I would tease them.

I would even call them out of their names using foul language. There I was, just daring them to try to make a better life for themselves. I was so caught up in my fear, in my anger and self-loathing and in my apathy that I couldn't even begin to understand how someone might find the strength to let go of the past and set a new course in life.

It wasn't until one day I found myself on their side of the fence in treatment, that I understood how my life could change.

Yes, that is correct! I found myself in treatment after I got caught for the last time calling folks out of their names.

I was approached by the Director of Treatment. She said to me, "Trina, It's one thing that you are afraid to get help, but do not stop those who want help."

"I'm not scared to get help; I just know it doesn't work," I replied. I said it with such authority and such a false sense of confidence. I wasn't going to back down.

"I tell you what," she said. "Let's make a deal. If you come to treatment for 30 days, I promise you that for the rest of your time here in jail I will make sure that you have a bottom bunk."

That incentive may not have seemed like much to some people, but to me, having a bottom bunk was like having a gold mine. I had come to jail for that first time all those many years ago being smaller than a telephone pole, but at that time in jail I weighed more than 400 pounds. Climbing in and out of a top bunk day after day isn't the most pleasant experience for any grown adult, but for someone in my poor physical health, it was agony.

I waited awhile before answering her. Over those next weeks, she would frequently find me.

"Have you made up your mind, chicken?" she would tease.

And one day I surprised even myself. I said yes. "I'll do it. I will be ready on Monday."

"Good," she said. "Make sure you say all your good byes and leave all your negative behavior behind, because this is a place of change."

I had feelings of fear creeping inside, and I knew this new challenge could go one of two ways:

- a) Inflate my ego, if I accomplished the goal, but leave me still living with criminal thinking and one-upmanship over others (but giving me all I thought I wanted, which was a comfortable bunk); or

- b) I would become the person that God intended me to be, which was loving, caring and considerate.

Jeremiah 3:16-17 is a statement that reflects this type of thinking which generally means, "Sometimes we stubbornly refuse to change because we are afraid we will miss the good old days, the hang out places, and the acquaintances. But when we surrender and give our life to God, His love will radically change our hearts, and these things will be missed less and less over time."

1. How would it feel to let go of some behavior or belief that is part of you (like being a tough bully, or a negative whiner) but that doesn't really help you?

_____

_____

2. What part of your old hangout will you miss if you dare to make a new, positive path?

_____

_____

3. What is something negative that you've said about yourself for a long time that makes you feel bad? Why do you say it about yourself?

_____

_____

4. What is something positive and uplifting about you that you know is who you are but perhaps you don't feel that you're worthy of believing it?

_____

_____

_____

Chapter 2 Homework Assignment:

A. What are you willing to let go of from your past walk of life?

_____
_____
_____
_____
_____
_____

B. How do you think you will feel if you let that go?

_____
_____
_____
_____
_____
_____

CHAPTER 3

In this chapter, we learn how Trina felt she had abandoned and neglected her children.

We review how, as a parent, our actions have impacted others.

We discuss what types of changes we can make to help not just ourselves but others who we love.

Finding The Parent Within Me

While I was in treatment, the Director of Treatment came to me to talk about my role as a mother. It was a role I hadn't taken enough responsibility for over the years. I knew I loved my children, but I was not able to take care of my own physical, spiritual and emotional needs, let alone take on mothering young babies. I was the one who also still needed mothering. And I wasn't alone. There were so many women incarcerated with me who were mothers who deeply loved their children but who couldn't provide the support to raise the kids in a healthy way.

The Director spoke to me very directly. "Trina, you are a very intelligent girl, and you have children who need to be taken care of. I want to see you make it, because there are people here who do not think you can make it in life. They believe you are going to spend the rest of your life inside these walls."

"That's not me. I'm not going to keep doing this," I said.

"Prove it then. Stop all the nonsense behavior, and focus on you, and getting out to care for your kids. Make a change for you."

Have you spent time thinking about the ways in which your children or your family have been affected by your criminal lifestyle? It isn't pleasant to think about the hurts that have been caused, but it is necessary to reflect on that. Maybe some of those loved ones have done things to you that were extremely hurtful – things you didn't deserve and didn't ask for. You might have blame, anger and even hatred inside of you. But those negative emotions are blocking you from receiving greater good in your life.

> *Our children are the ones who suffer the most. But they can heal, if we are able to help them, and show them that we are on a new path.*

As convicted felons, we have hurt people because of our actions. There are victims of our crimes, their families, society, and our own families. There is a large ripple effect that has touched so many people. And while we are incarcerated is the perfect time for us to start healing those wounds that are inside of us, and start helping others heal from the wounds we've given them.

Our children are the ones who suffer the most. But they can heal, if we are able to help them, and show them that we are on a new path.

We have to be willing to let them earn our trust back. It may be slow, because they don't want to be disappointed again by us. They might be afraid to depend on us, and that is natural for them to feel that way. We often can't depend on ourselves. But we have to start somewhere, and we can do it day by day by being willing to look honestly at where we have been, who we are today and what changes we are able to make.

1. Who are you willing to make changes in life for? _____

_____

_____

2. When you make changes for yourself, what will your life feel like as a result?

_____

_____

_____

3. How have your children's lives (or the lives of others close to you) been affected by your incarceration?

_____

_____

_____

4. When you make changes for others who you love, how might their lives be different as a result? _____

_____

_____

Chapter 3 Homework Assignment:

A. What changes do you really need to make? _____

_____

_____

_____

B. What help do you need in prison/jail and once you are out in order to make those changes? _____

_____

_____

_____

C. What is a plan to repair the relationship with your children, if that is part of your wish?

_____

_____

_____

CHAPTER 4

In this chapter we see how Trina was continuing to use her old street behaviors while she was in jail.

We start discussing the discipline that it takes to truly change.

We look at the relationships that need to change in order to help us move forward.

We assess what personal behaviors we may need to let go of in order to succeed.

Recognizing the Change That is Needed

Those days in treatment were active with classes, discussions, self-assessments and having to speak to others about our circumstances. I can remember Judges coming to visit the program, and my treatment director would make me be one of the residents who had to tell our personal life story. It felt good when they would commend me for trying to make a change. On one occasion, Thomas "Hollywood" Henderson, a famous NFL football player came to the jail to make a film on doing the right thing when nobody is looking. I was able to be a part of that film. I was beginning to believe some of the messages that I was hearing, and when I heard myself talk about change, I started to believe it might be possible, even for me.

But days were not easy in the program. As things began to move forward in treatment, I would struggle rising early enough to get to a first group meeting at 6:00 am. I was on medications to keep my emotions under control, and they led me to feel very tired and to sleep a great amount. And, of course, my health was pitiful because of the years of drugs and the excessive weight on my body. I didn't feel good physically most of the time. The treatment schedule was challenging also because I wasn't used to structure. It takes discipline to be committed to a program. I hadn't had a lifestyle that needed a lot of structure, so it was hard to meet the expectations that were placed on me.

I found myself instructing other women in the group to make my bed, do my laundry or other favors. I really believe they felt sorry for me. It seemed like a good deal for me, until someone called me on it and said I was still acting out my old behaviors. They said the only thing that was missing was the dope. They said I was acting like I was still dealing on the street, for instance, having people doing everything for me, when I could

> *At the core, it was my behaviors that were keeping me from changing.*

have been doing it for myself. After all, an important part of the treatment program was learning to be accountable to myself and to others for my actions and to be responsible.

When the others called me out on this behavior, the counselor was in the group discussion, so she decided to have a one-on-one conversation with me to confront the behavior also.

"Where ever we go, there we are" is a saying that really said a lot about me at the time. My behaviors followed me. They followed me on the streets back at home, and in the jail when I was misbehaving, and now even in treatment where I was attempting to do better. At the core, it was my behaviors that were keeping me from changing.

With the counselor, some of her first questions were about my childhood and how I was raised. I explained to her that I grew up in a somewhat decent home where my mother was responsible for raising her six kids. She worked herself to exhaustion so we would have shoes on our feet and food in our mouths. But there were too many other negative influences that crept in and made my brothers, sisters and me move away from the values our mother instilled in us. My mother's favorite saying to me was, "You didn't get bad until you got grown." I can attest to that.

1. Are there behaviors that you were taught (by family or friends) that no longer serve you well? If so, what are those behaviors? _____

_____

_____

_____

2. How would you go about letting go of those behaviors? _____

_____

_____

_____

3. Can you take your old attitude to the streets and expect a different outcome?

_____

_____

_____

_____

Chapter 4 Homework Assignment:

A. What are some descriptions of your unhealthy playmates – their attitudes and behaviors? _____

_____

_____

B. Who are your unhealthy playmates? List their first names only:

_____

_____

C. What existing relationships will stop you from growing into the person you want to be?

_____

_____

D. How will you stay away from those negatively-influenced relationships?

_____

_____

CHAPTER 5

In this chapter, Trina learns to start understanding the importance of setting goals and how to achieve them.

We focus on how to prioritize goals.

We assess what types of relationships we have in our lives.

Setting Personal Goals

This last time in jail, I started doing things differently. I surprised myself by finding that the treatment program was actually helping me break down some of the tough exterior. I was starting to see how my actions were sabotaging any chance of my success. I started thinking about future plans. Prior to my leaving, my counselor stated that I needed to write down my long-term goals and make short-term goals that I could actually accomplish. When we look back over our lives of destruction, most of us can say that we always wanted to accomplish something, and yet we failed.

The counselor helped me understand that having too many goals or goals that were too far out, such as 2 or 3 years, could overwhelm me. By being overwhelmed, it was likely that my goal would end up in the corner collecting dust.

My counselor asked me if I would allow her to see my goals. I had gained just enough belief in myself to share them with her. After looking them over, she stated that my priorities were out of order. You see, I first wanted to go see my family. Seeing my children wasn't an option at that time, because they had been taken from me. But I thought I needed to be with my brothers and sisters and other family who I had been with, even during those days of fighting and drugs.

She began to remind me how those people were not there for me while I had been incarcerated, and that they really hadn't been there for me on the streets. They had supported my illegal behaviors. She said that my first goal should be learning how to stay away from my old playmates (dope dealers, gamblers, thieves, prostitutes, addicted personalities, and old hang out spots), including my family.

Change brings on choices; and choices meant that I had to leave some things behind.

So while I thought I had a detailed list of goals, I was asked to trash it and start over. I was instructed to this time think of myself first.

> *What I found is that the people who assisted me in going to jail were not great candidates for me to hang out with...*

In making the new list of goals, I began to do a personal assessment of who and what I really needed in my life. What I found is that the people who assisted me in going to jail were not great people for me to hang out with when I got out unless they had made positive changes.

Can you remember the times that you were released, and each time you had a ride waiting for you at the nearest street corner? That ride probably took you to a couple of places, like to the dope strip (sell, buy, or trade), whore stroll, truck stop, or to report right back to your pimp. In one breath, you told yourself "I'm not going back to that lifestyle," but somehow you found yourself there once more.

I began realizing it wasn't a good idea to call those people who I used to call each time I got out to give me a pack of drugs to get me back up on my feet. Those people wouldn't really be able to assist me on my new journey.

Healthy relationships and supportive friends are necessary in order to make healthier choices. If we stand alone, we may fall short and become vulnerable to our dependencies and compulsiveness.

Without goals, there is no direction. I can't be prepared if I don't have a plan. And because goals help shape your relationships, it is so important to spend time thinking about what you want for your life and for your relationships with others. If you are only taking action without having an end-goal in mind, you may find that your life doesn't have as much purpose. And your life is here to be filled with purpose.

1. Do you have people who will help you get on your feet in a healthy way? List their first names and talk about why you trust them to be there for you.

_____

_____

_____

2. If you don't have healthy people in your life, what are a few things you can do to find those types of people, either while you are incarcerated or immediately upon release?

_____

_____

3. What are 5 goals that you really want to accomplish: (find safe place, get license, find job, etc.)?

_____

_____

_____

4. Do you need support to permanently stop gambling, stealing, using drugs or selling yourself? Where will you find these resources?

_____

_____

Chapter 5 Homework Assignment:

A. In the past, why do you believe you found yourself back at the same unhealthy spot? _____

_____

_____

B. What emotions do you feel when you think about those past choices?_____

_____

C. If you believe that you have no other means to survive, explain why you feel that way?

_____

_____

_____

D. What would it look like for you to be a survivor of your old lifestyle and to do things differently? _____

_____

_____

CHAPTER 6

In this chapter, Trina discusses moving from a place of feeling low to finding hope through a spiritual connection.

We will discuss how you can find positive people and activities while incarcerated to lift your spirits.

Finding Hope

Often times, I found myself feeling lonely and bored while serving time, so when the church groups would come by I would go to service just to get off the bunk. There were times when I did not feel like going and I would stay in my cell. One lady from the church group would come by and say "Come on, honey, the devil is a lie. We are not laying down on God's goodness."

The energy and passion that she shared was so amazing, there was nothing I could do but get up and join the group.

You see, there were times in my life that I felt like God had no place or space for me here on earth. There were times when I really felt like I had no more reason to live. But life would find its way back in, like when this little small church group blew hope back into me in those low times when I was missing my kids and my life outside the locked gates. I missed my old playmates and even the good times that ended up having me locked up.

But I can remember going to church one night and the lady said to us, "I want to see your face when you get out of here. I don't care if it is but one time." That gentleness did two things for me: 1) It showed that someone on the outside really did care, without a motive; 2) It gave me an understanding that help was available outside these walls.

> *But life would find its way back in, like when this little small church group blew hope back into me in those low times when I was missing my kids and my life outside the locked gates.*

Receiving that positive energy through the church was good for me. It really gave me the courage to start looking at some of the things I needed to change while serving this time.

Staying connected and centered around positive energy and groups such as volunteer organizations and church helped reduce my conflict with others while I was serving time. I admit that there were times when I disagreed with the decisions of the guards and in the past I would argue and talk back and would end up in detention or segregation. But as I continued to go into spiritual groups and being around uplifting people in the jail, I found myself feeling better and my spirit was lifted.

I found that the little girl in me wanted to grow up. I actually began singing hymns with people and we formed a choir. There were more than a dozen of us and we were able to perform for different groups in the jail. My spiritual journey, which was once lost due to drugs and addiction, was back on track. This was because of those volunteer groups who had faith in goodness of all things and faith in me. I looked forward to them coming and encouraging us. And so I began encouraging myself and others. I connected with a new level of inner spiritual faith, and it opened my heart.

As I found the courage to change and became more spiritually fed, I realized the decisions the guards were making were not as negative as I thought. I was able to start becoming a positive leader in the jail and helped resolve conflict. And my relationships with the guards were more respectful. And I even helped the guards and other inmates start resolving other issues.

1. Are you missing or grieving a part of your lifestyle that you know you need to change? _____

_____

_____

2. Have you experienced some low times or depression while doing time? What were they? _____

_____

_____

_____

3. What are some positive things that you'll be doing while doing your time? _____

_____

_____

_____

4. Who is giving you spiritual support? _____

_____

_____

Chapter 6 Homework Assignment:

A. How are you starting to forgive yourself? _____

_____

_____

_____

_____

B. What will it feel like when you forgive yourself completely?

_____

_____

_____

_____

CHAPTER 7

In this chapter, Trina is focusing on having an exit plan to help her do things differently.

This section is helping you make the preparation mentally to become truly free.

You are given the opportunity to begin thinking about practical resources you need upon release.

Finding an Exit Strategy on the Road to Release

I completed my treatment program. I was so proud of myself. My cellmates and the staff were proud of me also. It was one of the first times in my life when I completed something that made me feel like I could be something different than who I had been in the past.

And, an unexpected blessing was given to me while serving time. When the judge gave me my final sentence, he actually ordered me to a re-entry facility. Three days prior to my release, I was ordered to go to a women's two-year treatment center that had a halfway house component to it. Upon my release, the halfway house staff picked me up at "ROLL UP ONE" (the name of the final exit gate at my jail).

It was April 27th, 1997, and I can remember the officer's radios being dispatched to prepare for "ROLL UP ONE." Back then, when we were in our cells and other ladies were being released, we often would chant "free my people" when we heard them call for "ROLL UP ONE."

While I didn't have the authority to make the choice of where I wanted to go, I did have the choice of what I would do when I got there.

Looking back now, I realize I did not have an exit plan from jail. I believe that is the reason I continued to repeat the same lifestyle choices that kept returning me to jail. There's a saying that "insanity is doing the same thing over and over expecting different results." That's how I was living. I thought things would be different when I left jail each time, but I went to the same places, to the same people, had the same attitude and did the same behaviors. There's no chance I could have expected different and better outcomes.

> *While I didn't really have the authority to make the choice of where I wanted to go, I did have the choice of what I would do when I got there.*

When I say exit plan, what does that really mean? To me, it means knowing what can be done by you while you are incarcerated to start preparing at all levels for your release to freedom. What are you doing emotionally through counseling, prayer, strong communications and looking inward at yourself?

What are you doing physically to make your body healthier, so it has the strength to keep you moving forward? When your body feels bad, you won't be as motivated to keep going even when you face negative situations.

What are you doing from a practical planning standpoint to get ready for release? What are the resources you need? Who are the people you need and don't need in your life? What are the skills that will help you to succeed? What will that first week, the first 30 days, the first 90 and then 120 days look like for you? If you haven't thought it through and made a plan, then you'll likely end up repeating the same things you did before you were arrested.

Today, I spend time going back to the jails to share my story with men and women, and I always ask what their plan is when they walk through that last gate.

Most of the men and women I speak to just stare at me as if I told them they have no out date. Just like me when I was serving time, I was there to wait on an out date. Planning ahead was not on my radar. My only plans consisted of thinking how I would get out and meet up with my old playmates to exercise my old behaviors. My thoughts quickly went to getting one more hit, finding my way to dollars and engaging in a sex project. These actions just led me to live the life of hopelessness.

1. Do you have an exit plan? If yes, explain some parts of it. If not, tell why you don't have one.

_____

_____

_____

_____

2. What it will take for you to be ready to start creating an exit plan now?

_____

_____

3. What programs and action steps can you take while you are in prison to get you on a better path? _____

_____

_____

_____

4. Do you have an out date? If so, what is it? _____

5. Do you know where you need to go when your out-date arrives?

_____

6. Who will be there to pick you up? _____

7. Is that the best person for you during your first days of freedom? Why or why not?

_____

_____

_____

_____

8. Do you have people who will help you get on your feet in a healthy way? List their first names and talk about why you trust them to be there for you.

_____

_____

_____

_____

_____

_____

Chapter 7 Homework Assignment:

A. What will you do to get your license renewed, and what will you do for transportation?

_____

_____

B. Do you have legal fees, child support or other costs to pay back? If so, how can you make a sensible plan for these responsibilities?

    Legal Fees: _____

    Court Costs: _____

    Child Support: _____

    Driving Fines: _____

    Other: _____

_____

C. What are you hopeful about today? _____

_____

_____

Chapter 7 Homework Assignment:

D. What can you do to keep that hope alive once you get out?

_____
_____
_____
_____

E. What programs have you attended during incarceration? (List them) How may they help you upon release?

_____
_____
_____
_____
_____
_____

CHAPTER 8

In this chapter, Trina discusses barriers to employment and the reality of what it means to be free in society by being a productive citizen.

We will focus on understanding what your skills are and find work that allows these gifts to be used.

You will learn that there is something to be gained in every experience, and that with integrity and patience you can build a career.

Employment and Lifestyle Opportunities

The road to transition can be challenging, especially related to employment for felons.

I believe that most of us women and men have one major concern when we get out of prison or jail, and that is to make a living. Yet when I applied for jobs and tried to be honest on my applications, I was turned down because of my felony past. I allowed that rejection to lead me to the old lifestyle. The last time I was released, I was interviewed by a company that sold cleaning chemicals, and they hired disabled persons. I didn't share my criminal past. Yes, I lied and told them that I had a reading and a learning disability. I was hired.

But I had a learning experience there about integrity. I took some of

> *Being unemployed can lead us to make poor choices during our transition.*

the cleaner and hid it in a coke bottle one day to clean my own shoes. That wasn't honest of me and I shouldn't have done it. But I found out that that the chemical did not work. I realized that in treatment I had gained some level of integrity, and it didn't feel right working for that company after I noticed the chemical did not work. I felt like I was still the same old person who attested to have changed, yet I was calling on people to buy a chemical that did not work. So I immediately quit.

By this time I had been going to support meetings, and I told my support sponsor I had quit the job and my reason. I learned some good advice from her. While she understood my reason for leaving, she said that next time I considered quitting a job, I should have another already lined up. Being unemployed can lead us to make poor choices during our transition.

As felons, we often think we have to accept the low paying job, and though that may be part of the reality of society today it is not the only reality. There are increasingly more strong job opportunities for felons. Those jobs can protect us from making some other unfavorable decisions, like selling drugs or handing off sexual favors while trying to stay clean. We know that sometimes our criminal lifestyle felt like it gave us more material wealth and happiness, but at what cost?

Although freedom isn't free, what is the freedom of being able to sleep at night peacefully without guilt and waking up to be a productive citizen? For me, it is so comforting knowing that when I buy something, I've done it legally and no one can come after me and take it away. I have peace of mind today, and that feels completely free. And I don't have fear of losing my life or losing these items. And being a greater part of the whole of society and knowing that I am contributing to the good instead of filling society with pain and loss is so important for me.

What is our reality of peace and freedom and serenity? What does that look like for us who are felons? Can you even imagine what real freedom on the inside will be like for you when you start moving towards it? Let me tell you that it can feel truly amazing. And you deserve it.

After I was working at the chemical company and I knew it wasn't a long-term solution, I thought of a saying: "If you put as much energy into staying clean as you put into using, then you are guaranteed to have a successful recovery."

I thought about what skills I actually had in life. I remembered that I knew how to clean houses because I'd done that for drug dealers I'd worked with as an exchange for drugs. I started realizing that cleaning was a skill of mine. So, it took a lot of courage and the support of my partner, but I decided to make a flyer promoting a personal cleaning business, and I took it to a few local businesses. I started talking to businesses, and pretty soon I had a few businesses and house owners who asked my partner and me to clean. What was amazing is that we were successful and it felt great! We started spending wisely and were even able to save money.

Eventually, I quit my other job and made the cleaning service my full-time career. And it was a few years later that we decided to invest money into a halfway house and named it *Mending Hearts*.

1. Are you addicted to the money or the lifestyle? _____

_____

_____

2. How does it feel thinking about going back to that lifestyle?

_____

_____

_____

3. What employment skills do you have that could help you start a healthy career? _____

_____

_____

_____

4. Where could you begin looking for employment? _____

_____

_____

_____

Chapter 8 Homework Assignment:

A. Do you have clothing when you leave incarceration?

_____

_____

B. What does your current housing situation look like (be honest)?

_____

_____

C. If that housing situation isn't reliable or healthy, what alternatives can you find in the short-term?

_____

_____

D. Are there education needs that you desire?

_____

_____

_____

CHAPTER 9

In this chapter, Trina experiences the desire to go back to the old lifestyle to earn money, but she's supported by healthy friends.

We understand the reality that not every day will be easy, but we can stay true to our self and overcome our fears.

Having support is key, because it holds us accountable.

Being Honest With Ourselves

I can remember getting out and being at the halfway house and having the thoughts of selling drugs again. I had a bright idea that if I sold a couple of packs (drugs) that I would have enough money to pay my halfway house rent, get the kids some clothes, and get an apartment so that I could get the kids back. I was living with guilt because my oldest child would say that I didn't love her and her siblings because I wouldn't let them live with me. That was pressure that I put on myself, feeling like I wasn't the mother I needed to be.

Sometimes it felt like I was a pot on the stove and my lid was just about to tip over. Thankfully, I had an old pal who watched out for me. She knew I was up to something because I was not the same, and usually when I got home to the halfway house she and I would discuss our day and prepare for a group meeting. She saw that I had been stressed and crying about my kids. On one particular night, this friend could tell I was really vulnerable and weak. Before I could get out of the halfway house to try and use my old talents, she had called my sponsor. In no time, there were three or four cars lined up in front of the halfway house,

> *Sometimes it felt like I was a pot on the stove and my lid was just about to tip over.*

and those friendly supporters got out of their vehicles playing music from artist R. Kelly, *"I Believe I Can Fly."*

My sponsor grabbed me by the hand. I knew she was worried.

"What are you about to do, Trina?"

"Go see my family."

"When did you decide that?"

"Well, I've been thinking about it." I didn't want to tell her how hard things were.

"Ok, I'll take you over there and then we'll go to a meeting."

Instantly my heart began pounding, and I said to her, "No, you don't need to be over there, because they are still using."

She said, "I know, remember you told me all about them. I didn't think you wanted to be around them, what has changed?"

I began to rumble some lame excuse. Then she asked, "Are you trying to get high or do you think that a monkey can sell bananas?"

She continued on. "Do you think you are strong enough to go sell dope and stay clean?"

I said yes. In my twisted thinking at that moment, I thought I could sell and not go back into active addiction.

"What is it that you are needing?" she asked.

I began telling her all that I needed, like money for food and clothes for the kids, so I could eventually bring my children home.

She said, "I tell you what. Go pay your rent, and I will buy you whatever you want and need."

I explained how tired I was and how deflated I felt in my state of poverty.

She kept encouraging me with her words of faith. "Trina, if you continue to pay your rent at the halfway house then God will bless you with your own apartment and then from your apartment He will give you the ability to have a mortgage."

I didn't believe her. I didn't feel I deserved that level of goodness, and I didn't know if I was strong enough to keep the faith.

She stayed with me and encouraged me to just try to do the right thing. I told her I would try. And I did try. I kept paying that rent. I kept living from a place of faith. And eventually she came back to ask me what I wanted and needed, and I realized I didn't really need anything. I could think of nothing! I mean nothing!

1. Do you have a problem being responsible? _____

_____

_____

2. What does your life look like when you aren't being responsible?

_____

_____

_____

3. Do you need an accountability partner and what would you want that person to do for you?

_____

_____

4. Is there someone you already know who could be that partner? List his or her first name.

_____

_____

_____

Chapter 9 Homework Assignment:

A. If you don't know anyone now to hold you accountable, what steps could you take to find someone either now or once you are released? _____

_____

_____

B. What therapy or support do you need when you leave to assist you from "your old stinking thinking?"

_____

_____

C. Where will you go to receive medical treatment or get medication if it's needed? _____

_____

D. Is there a 12 step program for you (drugs, gambling, food, sex, stealing, co-dependency)? Where will you find it?

_____

_____

CHAPTER 10

In this chapter, Trina reflects on some of her early mistakes related to dating and finances, but finding courage to keep going.

We focus on the importance of avoiding mistakes by finding a plan that works for us – and that plan has a lot of different parts.

Seeing your own value and working on yourself is an important part of your journey.

Staying Strong and On the Path

At that point in my transition, I was still fresh out of jail and wanted to prove to people that I had changed and that I was not going back. And I had promised my kids that I would be there for them as well. I think about how many times I had told them to trust me, but then I let them down. This time, I really wanted it to be different.

We know that family can be a major trigger for any of us who have been incarcerated. There was no way I could take care of my kids because I had not learned to take care of myself at that point. No matter how much I loved them, I needed to experience what it was like to love myself. I still had some healing to do, and the halfway house was giving me the time and space to do that.

As I look back now, I realize that in order to take care of myself, I should have spent more time thinking about my own physical health and wellness. I could have gone to the doctor more for checkups, I could have begun exercising and taken quiet time for me. Even for my emotional needs, I could have found more counselors to help me with my stress and guilt. And I could have found experts to help me learn to budget my money.

> *We know that family can be a major trigger for any of us who have been incarcerated.*

Have you considered your personal wellness plan? What is the most important aspect of your own wellness? Is it your physical health or your emotional state of mind? Remember that there are so many sources for you. You can find a gym. You can begin walking daily. You can let go of too much fast foods. And you can find support groups and health professionals.

I think of some of the mistakes I made early, along the way: dating more than one person; making guilt payments to my kids; and getting in a relationship with a using addict.

We all are going to make mistakes on our road to recovery, but some of these mistakes can be avoided if we look ahead to the end result instead of only at what is right in front of us.

At the end of the day, looking back I believe that we find ourselves in these difficult situations due to the lack of confidence in God's will for us. As a result, we experience consequences like dishonesty, drunkenness, violence, family problems, irresponsibility, greed, lust, money issues, hatred, and dependence of others to care for us.

So as we prepare to exit into a life worth living, we must remind ourselves of the things that keep us trapped, lonely and hopeless, yet reach for the sky in the things we know that have been promised to us such as life, love and limitless possibilities.

1. What does it feel like when you place pressure on yourself believing that you need to take care of someone else before you take care of yourself? _____

_____

_____

2. What are the emotional and physical dangers of you taking care of others when you aren't taking care of you? _____

_____

_____

3. What promises have you made to loved ones and friends that you're not sure you can keep? _____

_____

_____

4. How do you feel about these promises? _____

_____

5. What promise do you know for certain you can make for yourself today? _____

_____

EXIT PLAN

Chapter 10 Homework Assignment:

A. What are the primary triggers that might lead you back to drugs, sex or other criminal behaviors? _____

_____

_____

_____

B. What are several actions you can take when you feel those negative triggers threatening your success?

_____

_____

_____

C. In what ways do you love yourself? _____

_____

_____

_____

CHAPTER 11

Your Personal Final Release Plan:

As part of your final preparation for release, you will want to prepare yourself for those first critically-important days of freedom.

It's suggested that you use all the materials you've prepared in this handbook to help you complete your Personal Final Release Plan. This Release Plan will be especially important in those first days and weeks of freedom.

Personal Final Release Plan

Primary Community Contact

Name

Relationship

Phone   Email

Address

Will you be on Probation/Parole? ❏ Yes ❏ No

Contact Person Name:

Phone   Email

Identification

Do you have: ❏ Birth Certificate?   ❏ Social Security Card?   ❏ State ID?

If No, where will you go to aquire these? _____

Who can assist you if you don't know how to acquire these?_____

Departure from Incarceration

Who is picking you up when you are released?

Name _____

Relationship _____

Contact Information _____

Where will you live week 1? _____

Where will you live the first 3 months? _____

If at Transitional Housing, list name: _____

    Address _____

    Contact person _____   Phone number _____

    Interview Date _____   Accepted Date _____

Transportation

How will you get to work once you have employment? _____

_____

Do you have a valid drivers' license? ❏ Yes ❏ No

If no, explain any plans if you seek to gain a license? _____

_____

Clothing and Food

Where will you get clothing? _____

_____

Where will you get food? _____

_____

Government Assistance

What type of government assistance (food stamps, disability, etc) might you apply for? _____

_____

Where and when will you go to apply for these? Date, Location, etc.

_____

_____

Health Services
MENTAL HEALTH:
Where will you go? _____

How will you pay? _____

Appointment: _____

Case Manager/Doctor name and contact information

_____

EXIT PLAN

MEDICAL HEALTH:

Where will you go? _____

How will you pay? _____

Appointment: _____

Case Manager/Doctor name and contact information

_____

Finances and Employment

How will you support yourself financially until you have a job? _____

_____

_____

_____

What career services programs will you use? Name of Agency, Address and Contact Information: _____

_____

_____

Date of Appointment: _____ Do you have a resume? ❏ Yes ❏ No

If no, what services will you use to create one? _____

_____

Education

Current education level: _____

Do you plan to continue education? _____

If Yes and if this is immediate, list the steps you will take to pursue this and any contact information: _____

_____

_____

Social Network

Positive personal support, family, friends, sponsor, mentor:

Name _____

Relationship _____

Phone _____ Email _____

Address _____

Name _____

Relationship _____

Phone _____ Email _____

Address _____

Social Network (Continued)

Name _____

Relationship _____

Phone _____ Email _____

Address _____

Name _____

Relationship _____

Phone _____ Email _____

Address _____

Name _____

Relationship _____

Phone _____ Email _____

Address _____

Name _____

Relationship _____

Phone _____ Email _____

Address _____

Community Programs

List all programs or services in the community you may attend to help you in your reentry (church, AA/NA, aftercare or other support meetings):

Name of Agency/Organization
_____

Location
_____

Dates and Times of Services
_____

Transportation for you to attend?
_____

Name of Agency/Organization
_____

Location
_____

Dates and Times of Services
_____

Transportation for you to attend?
_____

Name of Agency/Organization
_____

Location
_____

Dates and Times of Services
_____

Transportation for you to attend?
_____

Community Programs (Continued)

Name of Agency/Organization
_____

Location
_____

Dates and Times of Services
_____

Transportation for you to attend?
_____

Name of Agency/Organization
_____

Location
_____

Dates and Times of Services
_____

Transportation for you to attend?
_____

Name of Agency/Organization
_____

Location
_____

Dates and Times of Services
_____

Transportation for you to attend?
_____

Name of Agency/Organization
_____

Location
_____

Dates and Times of Services
_____

Transportation for you to attend?
_____

Children

List children if you have them _____

_____

_____

_____

_____

What will your visitation/custody arrangements be? _____

_____

_____

_____

Where are they living now and where will they live? _____

_____

_____

_____

FINAL THOUGHTS

How I Made It

Twenty years later, I look back on those days in jail and in the halfway house, and then at my life afterwards that was focused on sobriety, living with honesty and regaining trust in my close relationships. I knew how to sell drugs, but I did not know how to live without them. I had to learn what that life looked like.

I made it through those dark days, and I believe that you can, too. We all can heal from our past and create a new life of meaning.

Here's How I Made It:
- I had a praying mamma.
- I stayed teachable.
- I took a chance on something different than what I already knew.
- I trusted in other women who had been where I had been and who were living successfully.
- I began to hang with people who were doing positive things in life (they are called winners).
- I prayed to God with prayers like, "Show me how to live a new lifestyle. God, teach me how not to lie to myself."
- I surrendered.

Things I resisted:

1. Using drugs, in any form
2. Going back to the old playground
3. Calling on those supposed friends who let me down
4. Hanging out on the old block
5. Trying to show everybody I'm better

My hope for you is that you find real peace, joy and love in your freedom. Reflect on these positive action steps, and know that you are worthy of all the good that will come to you.

1. Pray for direction
2. Be confident and know where you will call home
3. Gain courage to say 'No' to unhealthy behaviors and people
4. Be willing to ask for help in your most vulnerable times
5. Be willing to see yourself with a new set of eyes

May this book be a resource to remember that there is a way out with prayer, planning and participation. And when you find that way out, consider reaching back and helping someone else.

One of my golden rules is not to leave any place or situation without a destination. Now that you see your journey ahead of you, let your journey begin.

"May we continue to do the right thing no matter who's looking."

www.ingramcontent.com/pod-product-compliance
Lightning Source LLC
Chambersburg PA
CBHW080417300426
44113CB00015B/2551